FRUITFUL CHAOS

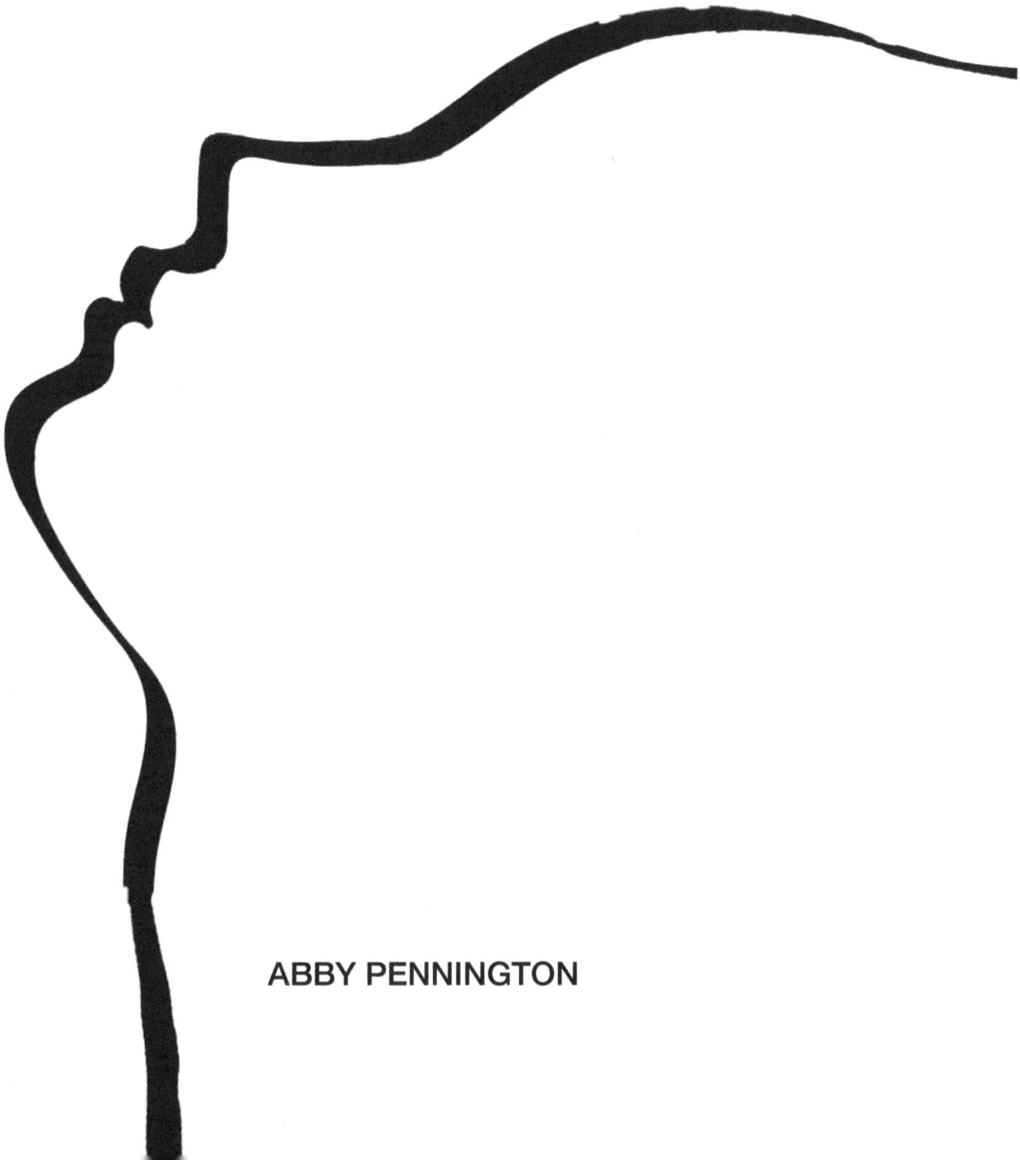

ABBY PENNINGTON

Contact the author at the following:
Email: abbyg.pennington@gmail.com
Instagram: abbypenningtonpoet & abbygpennington

Book and graphic design by Carl Pennington, 212films.com
Edited by Abby Pennington

First Printing, 2024
ISBN 979-8-218-40774-2

Printed in the United States of America

These are words from my darkest moments
This was my pain
But, I made it through
And you can too
You are not alone

My eyes are always open
for sleep never comes
my heart is always racing
for peace never stays
I've learned to love
my brokenness
as it is
for it is the reason
I am a writer
my mental battles
are the thorn
in my flesh
that gives me
the words
to tell my story
of fruitful chaos

The fireflies dance
with a glow
a joyous light
I've always wanted
to feel the magic
burst forth
from within
beckoning wonder
the mesmerizing glory
of a sacred symbol
not to lose hope
May they brighten
my path
and lead me
to the enchantment
of lasting happiness
so that my skin illuminates
and I dance
underneath the sky of stars
beaming down on me
The moonlit charm
of fireflies
electrify my soul
to overpower the darkness
with light

In the dark
of the night
I am awake
a nocturnal soul
unlike the others
They hide
from the beasts
under the bed
but I throw back
the covers
and come out
to dance
with them

My mind is chaos
a black hole
of endless thoughts
broken fragments
dreams and desires
unattainable wishes
stored and cherished
kept in secret
as if someday
I'll find the key
to put back together
the crushed soul
locked inside
but until then
a vortex
of pandemonium
replaces my brain

Got tired
of talking
and not being heard
so I write
because at least
the pages
want to hear
what my heart
has to say

Voices in the mind
like a crowd of people
all yelling
shouting at you
wanting to change you
and reshape the elements
that uniquely make you
like no matter what's done
can never be good enough
appearance and personality
every aspect
not suiting to the standards
those voices heard
are real
came from the ones
who created the lies
you learned to believe
that you must succumb
to the rest of the world
think "normal" thoughts
act as a manicured puppet
speak with tape across the mouth
look like the structured stereotype
society has created
to follow their rules
but instead
I dare you
to make your own rules

I've been trying
to swim away
from the past
but the waves
are rough
and I'm gasping
for air
trying not to drown
under the pressure
of all my pain
and sorrows

They look happy
in the light
I remember
what it felt like
a sheer fabric
drifting delicately
around me
softly kissing my skin
that was the light
but I don't feel it
not anymore
instead heavy weights
rest on my shoulders
a burden so demanding
that my knees buckle
under the pressure
my heart races
my mind tells me
to give up
that is the darkness
and since it is
my present reality
I envy their smiles
and yearn to take
from them
the light
I once had

If someone
could ever
love me
for my crazy
then maybe
I could
love me
for my body
because
the figure
I see
in the mirror
is broken
and needs
the other half

The mind is a prison
thoughts are chains
entrapping those who dare
to let madness guide them
allow feelings to take control
like the addictive taste
of alcohol stinging the throat
the voices will latch on
to begin a cycle
of unquenchable thirst
no escaping the chaos
that stabs the heart
creating the desire
to ease the pain
to erase the cravings
like downing a bottle
then finishing a second
repeated cycles
voices, thoughts, chains
the struggle for liberty
of one's own mind
no more sense
just mad

Tonight I don't want to
go out in a crowd
just want to
sit under the stars
listen to Sinatra
smoke the cigarettes
drink the wine
without interruption
maybe later
I'll open my journal
and write a poem
about you
how you persisted
to get me out
but I find
loneliness to be
a wicked friend
some nights I love him
some nights I hate him
right now
I love the thrill
of sitting alone
and realizing
this poem
is about you
so even when
I'm alone
I still think
about you
and that's when
I hate loneliness
like I do now

I've danced
with death before
luckily
his bad taste
in music
scared me
away

The instability
I've always known
keeps me going for
bad relationships
as if I expect
to never get off
the rollercoaster
as if the ups and downs
have become comfortable
as if I expect my
fate to be
like my parents
never knowing if
the love is real
always wondering
if the love
will come today
and leave tomorrow
maybe someday
I'll stop the ride
and stand on flat ground
with someone who's
brave enough
to show me
what true love
actually looks like

Why would I keep quiet
when there are millions
of influencing voices
in my head
every moment
surges waves of ideas
making a tsunami of disarray
the mind never rests
so many thoughts
ought I gone mad
from the mob
or speak out
maximize expression
tell those who judge
"It's ok to be crazy
not to go insane"

I can feel the art flow
like majestic vibrations within
the taste of colors electrify
to become new shaped oddities
belonging to an abstract realm
I find myself in a psychedelic dream
lost in a distorted wonderland
where the road ahead is behind
upside down is right side up
a spinning mind of madness
no recollection of time
but words yes
finding words with color
picturesque happenings
in a frame or in a box
trapped within dimensions
a race with no course
clock without numbers
fallen captive to insanity
help but don't save me
save but don't rescue me
I fell down a hole
a long way gone
I'm wet, but I'm dry
I'm cold, but I'm hot
in the air, but I'm on the ground
in the art, but I created it

Spiraling down
the dark tunnel
of despair
no hope left
only misery
fueled with erosion
by corruptive behavior
slashes in skin
pills in mouth
smoke in lungs
empty stomach
little bones
self-destruction
caused by the mind
the cruel world
showed a knife
an appealing glint
to end the struggle
but the decision
would make a claim
either give up
and die as a victim
or fight
and live as
a strong soldier

The desperate drunkard
searching hungrily
for their beloved
a full bottle
the treasure
to fill emptiness
which devours sense
trying to ease the void
by flooding their blood
with painkiller
with escape medicine
anything to drown out
all the emotions
every memory
lost in a tidal wave
a torrent of liquor
and a finished bottle
reminds them
of their soul
gone
pit in the stomach
as if death reoccurred
and they lost
the one who
used to occupy
the space
now filled
with alcohol

Tired of
playing charades
the second I
trust someone
they change
character
and leave me
guessing where
they went
and who they
are now

That glorious feeling
of sunlight
tenderly beaming
upon my skin
makes me smile
glad I chose
to stay
and breathe
the fresh air
instead of leaving
because of letting
the thin air
of destruction
choke me to death
The sunlight
is like my
newfound hope
and I swathe
my beaten body
with its layers
of warmth
to heal
all the wounds
brought upon
before I found
the natural cure

So empty inside
yet walls are closing in
feeling suffocated
panicking from fears
drowning in abyssal sorrow
there is no escape
from the pit of despair
the past infliction of hurt
shattered into pieces
a broken figure
barely breathing
a negative rope
tied around the neck
gone to the point
of purple flesh
rotten bones
sunken skull
the lies that killed
a dead mind
the whispers that killed
a dead mind
buried
before the grave

Rules aren't for me
tell me not to
and I will
because rebellion
ignites my soul
with fiery passion
so don't bother
with the lecture
I tune out the words
I don't want to hear
blame it on age
blame it on parents
or accept the nature
of the beast
within me
didn't you know
he's in you too
it's why you judge me
when you have
problems of your own
fix your issues
and don't try
to fix me
I am what I am
like it or not

To the voices
in my head
I scream out
enough torture
my broken mind
cannot survive
for much longer
until the darkness
finishes eating
the last piece
of sanity

I want to love myself
I want to spread love
and be in love
and feel loved
just for my life
to be overflowing
with love
so that the sadness
can't reach me
any longer
but the problem is
I put up
too many walls
so the love
tries to enter
but the despair
trapped inside
won't let love in

Poor fool
sitting outside
late at night
trying to get drunk
not caring about
the smoke
in my lungs
trying to ease
the pain of the fact
that nothing good
seems to last
happiness is fleeting
like all the relationships
I've seen and had
so I lie to myself
like the poor fool
believing that I'm better
off being alone
but really
I'm crippled by the fact
that I couldn't
have us be
the one thing
in my life
that lasted

Too much in her mind
scattered thoughts
anxious and stressed
build and grow
until her head cracks
bleeding out the chaos
until her heart blows
splattering out the strain
had no control
over the constant worry
the continual despair
and what followed
the fear and hatred
looking in the mirror
seeing a broken figure
nothing but disgust
for how weak and vulnerable
that body became
to the lies within
scattered thoughts
the inner demons spoke
to her fragile state
and she fell captive
to their torture
in her head

The manipulation
combined with
the opinions
is enough
to make me
drink myself
away
so that
my liver
is flooded
so that
I drown
and don't
awake
to hear
their voices
again

The pills
feel like a lump
in my throat
a reminder
that I wasn't
strong enough
to fight on my own
so I take them
desperately seeking a cure
even if it contorts me
into deeper distress
the risk is worth
the chance of making it
on the other side
when I can finally
come alive
again

No one can see
that there is
more beneath
my smile
unless they choose
to look deep enough
to see the pain
in my eyes
and those that do
always ask what's wrong
but I might have
no answer because
that pain in my eyes
is damage from the past
and while I have
healed from the past
there are permanent wounds
that I might never
be able to fix
but I've learned
to be at peace
with the pain
because I know
it's made me stronger
and given me
depth and wisdom
to know that
the ones who
really understand
won't accept the smile
or seek a problem
to fix
they'll look me
in the eyes
and say nothing
but we'll feel
a little less alone

Maybe I am
better off
alone
because love
lead to hurt
and caused
the madness
which lead to
the drunkenness

I was born with
these crooked bones
in my spine
the lower part
of my back
and as the years
have passed
I've had injuries
far too many
that have beaten me down
made me realize
how fragile I am
and I hate it
I hate the constant
levels of pain
sometimes I wake up
to the stabbing
to the throbbing
to the punching
in my back
protesting at having
to function
I've had sleepless nights
collapses on the floor
unable to move
can't breathe
because the pain
is so bad

(cont.)

and no one
really unsterstands
how torturous it is
to take all those pills
and still feel it
so a lot of times
when my mind was a mess
and I did get drunk
it was really just
because nothing else
could take away the pain
except the escape
from reality
on the edge
of drunkenness
when my body
went numb

The opinions
the lectures
the disapproval
is enough
to make one
go mentally insane
but learning
not to care
realizing
that individuality
never needed approval
and being yourself
is the only way
to freedom
the only way
to not go crazy
is to let go
spread those wings
you hide
and fly

In my brain
there is a spider
that weaves
webs of chaos
between each thought
I try to kill it
but I can never
put an end
to the pest
It lays eggs
and the babies
of madness hatch
to creep and crawl
within my whole body
so I scratch
my skin raw
until the voices
subside
If they ever do
maybe I won't
want to disappear
with the spider

I'll put on
the smile
fake the laugh
hold back
the tears
swallow the pain
and say
I'm okay
to remain
the strong
independent human
I tell myself
I have to be

My thoughts
are swirling
like my mind
is spinning
I feel out
of control
but the escape
of the high
has numbed
the feeling
of pain
you caused me

The outward appearances
do not reveal
a person's depth
You see me
and think I'm strong
you judge my life
as better than yours
that's the problem
with human nature
comparison is common
but beyond what's seen
inside I am fighting
barely able not to break
to hold myself together
when I'm alone
I cry gallons of tears
drowning in my emotions
and the fact
that you admire me
when I really
just pretend to be ok
and act tough
to hide the truth
it pains me
even more to know
that if I was honest
you wouldn't understand

I tried not to
fall for you
because you were
sure to leave
Of course
you left
and I cried
all these tears
over you
Now there's nothing
left except
numbness
and a cold
wounded heart

The feelings and emotions
are hard to understand
I'm always confused
and indecisive
but I found
that when I drink
I like myself better
because the mayhem
settles down
into a peaceful quiet
a tipsy slumber
a comforting buzz
the voices I hear
all cease to exist
when I drown
them out
with liquor
I can finally hear
the truth

I hate looking back
at those pictures
the smiles seem foreign
those bright hopeful eyes
long forgotten
in the mirror
the one who looks back
can't be the same person
in the photos
because the reflection I see
wears a frown of misery
and stares with eyes of despair
that snapshot figure
feels like a fake
though once happiness existed
where did it go
why does the present face
not match the past one
how could I
forget how to smile
and look at the memories
as if they weren't
my own

What a wicked
little daydream
you were
creeping into
my every thought
acting like you
wanted to stay
but really
it was all
just a game
you played
and once you won
you took the trophy
and ran with it
adding to your collection
of minds you've stolen
and hearts you've broken

Most nights lately
I come home
after midnight
and drink
to not feel anything
I've gotten to a point
where I get annoyed
with feelings
because they come
tied to expectations
and I've learned
not to expect anything
because I've been
let down
too many times
so the alcohol
is a way of
telling the feelings
to fuck off

I curse my own name
falling for the one
who will never
love me back
How could I be
so ignorant
to think that love
would find me
Unrequited
but I still had
the slightest hope
a child I was
believing in fairytales
when they aren't real
I should have known
what's too good
to be true
is a loss
and so I sit
here alone
with the fragments
of the memories
we once had
and let them
slip away
from my daydreams

Exhaustion overpowers
my ability to live
a drained body
that aches to move
a restless mind
that throbs to think
a pounding heart
that burns to work
every function
is hindered
by chronic fatigue
but I brought it
upon myself
letting the pressure
of the world
sit on my back
creating the stress
that shouldn't exist
being the origin
of my sorrow
so no matter
how much I sleep
I'll never feel awake
until I let go
of the load
and breathe again

In the concrete jungle
with a top hat
and cigarette
going in and out
of jazz bars
trying all the wine
drunk in a room
full of people
to hide the loneliness
behind a fake smile

You have it all
the wants
and the needs
but you're still unhappy
with the profitable job
you feel trapped
in the large house
you feel empty
with your own family
you feel lonely
no matter how much
you continue to gain
satisfaction never lasts
the superfluities
continue their corruption
because you adhere
to finding happiness
in materialistic pleasures
Don't you realize now
that being rich
can make you poor
that less is more
because less
leaves more room
for joy to move in

I'm the messed-up kid
my parents tried too hard
trying to shape me
to be who they wanted
but it was never enough
because I'm far from it
I curse
and they tremble
I smoke
and they cry
I'm depressed
and they're angry
wondering why
I turned out wrong
and can't get
my life right
but I'd be doing better
if they'd stop
trying to fix me
and let me
be me
I guess it's time
not to care
anymore
because I can't let
their expectations
continue to drive me
mad

Giving up seems
so much easier
than constantly fighting
all the battles
in my mind
they were enough
to break me apart
and shatter me
to unfixable pieces
so that recovery
would be impossible
but this is why
I continue to fight
the slight hope
of being the victor
the one standing
in the end
healed and strengthened
from the scars
able to look back
and be proud
of the soldier
I became
when this day comes
I can finally put the gun down

Do you ever
just wish
for a break
For life to take
its hands off
of your throat
and stop
smothering you
so you can
breathe again

You promised
not to lie
knowing that
I'd been lied to
a lot in my life
yet you made
me believe
the biggest lie
of all:
That you wanted me
Just as soon
as I fell for it
you turned into
a ghost
and let me
fall out of
your hands
with all the
broken promises

Always the thoughts
and the cigarettes
and the alcohol
and the tears
and the pain
all of it combined
spilled together
put into words
and called poetry
because I let
the madness
of this life
break me down
enough to where
the only option
I had was
to write
in order to
save myself

Teach me how
to smile again
I forgot
what it feels like
when the corners
of my mouth
lift up
and my lips
spread apart
and my teeth
display glee
My face has not
expressed anything
other than a frown
for far too long
and if it did
I wouldn't remember
the fake smiles
No, I need
to smile
and feel it
spread through
my entire body
with tingles
of euphoria
that actually
tell the truth
that actually mean
I'm happy
once more

I'm grateful
for my brother
because
he's the reason
that mom has
at least
one kid
going somewhere
in life

Stuffing down stress
by overeating
I thought it would help
the distraction of chewing
the pleasure of tasting
but now I look
in the mirror
feeling miserably full
seeing extra skin
chunky waist
thick thighs
and saggy arms
I want to throw up
want to starve myself
as punishment
for what I've done
because I didn't
solve the problem
I just made
a bigger one

Confusion
I can't seem
to escape it
one day
something feels right
the next
it feels wrong
like no matter
how hard
I try to solve
my life puzzle
the pieces
never fit
and I'm always
searching for answers
questioning my purpose
if nothing works
then I am
a broken soul
never meant to be
fixed

Found myself
banking off the sadness
seeing gray clouds
on a sunny day
and every little thing
I can find wrong
annoys me
and my coffee tastes
watered down
like my soul that is thirsty
for more life and flavor
Here it is again
sinking back under
into the abyss
of depression
where not even the cigarettes
I smoke
have the decency
to make me smile
anymore

To feel
or not to feel
that is the question
I ask myself
whenever I want
a drink
and most nights
I end up drunk
at the same bar
numb inside

The money I spend
on medication
could be used for gas
but when my car
runs close to empty
it reminds me
that I'm already there
so the fuel I need
takes the shape
of a pill
and that pill
and its friends
will hopefully be enough
to fill my tank up
to give my body
the energy it lacks
the happiness it's missing
I guess the meds
are more important
than the car
until I run out of gas
and can't drive
to get the pills
then both tanks
are completely empty
left bone dry

Got high today
because it was
your birthday
and my mind
was reliving
all the moments
I had with you
but I know
you don't care
you never did
otherwise
it wouldn't have been
so easy
for you
to walk away

Don't fuck around
with careless words
they are more
than letters and sound
words are feelings
that create thoughts
in their mind
and those thoughts
can be so cruel
from those words
you spoke
that not only
did you cause
a mind mayhem
to take place
your words pierced
into their skin
and left behind
wounds so deep
that the aftermath
revealed the scars
of self-harm
be careful
what you speak
because you could
be the culprit
of those scars

No matter where I go
they look right through me
as if I were invisible
maybe they can sense
the sorrow that's stuck
in my chest
it's lodged in
as if I were
shot by an arrow
maybe they can see the arrow
but are too afraid
to acknowledge it
or maybe I have fallen
into a hole so dark
that my soul died
and I am nothing more
than a ghost

Tonight the only
way to cope
was to numb myself
with alcohol
and cigarettes
because I'm just
too fucking tired
of trying
always fighting
mentally and physically
trying not to break
but this curse
of feeling like
I'm dying inside
has its grip
on me
too tight
and I'm just
too fucking tired

Every time I start something
or partake in newness
I feel like I must run
turn back and leave
The anxiety in my chest
is fear in my brain
and it's so easy
to fall into the trap
of being too scared to try
of thinking I'm not good enough
or feeling the restlessness
build up within me
and turn into hatred
loathing the places I go
the people I meet
all because I feel trapped
in my own skin
with these trembling bones
that don't accept
one small failure
that can't bear
one look of disapproval
the nervous delirium
makes me quit
before I truly begin
and I wonder
if I'll ever achieve
those longed for dreams
when I can't even control
the anxiety haunting my mind
and wrecking my life
into severe havoc
so it seems
my fate is
to be anxiety's
eternal prisoner

Drinking my days away
until you find me
and give me
a reason to live
out of intoxication
because I'm only here
to feel the burn
in my mouth
to feel the sting
in my throat
it's the only way
I can survive
by drowning out the past
flooding out the voices
with liquor and shots
the bars and the people
like addictive drugs
to mask my reality
with something better
please come and save me
be that something better
I need rehabilitation
through your love

It's hard to be
alone in silence
because you must face
what might be
the greatest enemy
of all…
your mind
and all its
chaotic thoughts

I've always been told
who I should be
what structure to follow
what status to claim
and as a young kid
I knew they were wrong
freedom is not
being made into a machine
or morphed into a prototype
the common strive to be rich
would never grant happiness
being an entrepreneur
or a deskman
would not achieve
my treasured aspirations
so I threw away
their box-like standards
because it caused
the downward spiral
of my mental health
I had to learn
how to follow
the desires of my heart
and whether they approved
I had to not care
because I'd rather die
as a free soul
than as a puppet
on their strings

You don't have to
break my heart
I did it for you
with my own
doubts and insecurities
sabotaging the hope
I had in us

Depression tells me
I'll always be alone
and most of the time
it seems true
though I'd like to believe
I can be social again
but first I'll have to
be positive again
because no one wants
a broken soul
a sorrowful spirit
a drained body
as a friend
no one wants
half a person
as a lover
and I understand
because even I
don't want me
anymore
I need to find
the half of me
depression took away
so I'll no longer be
lonely

They probably think
I'm crazy
for the things
that I do
but for me
nothing speaks
exhilaration
more than
having people
think I'm crazy
for the things
that I do

There is no longer
a healthy balance
in my appetite
somedays I overeat
stuffing the food down
as if it would alleviate
all the stress
but afterward
I feel worse
and hate myself more
other days I starve
letting the emptiness
in my stomach
be the example
of the sorrow
and vacancy
in my heart
letting my bones
feel the malnourishment
as punishment
for the binges
and negative thoughts
It feels like
there is no escape
I either deserve the food
or deserve the hunger
the only cure
is to rid of the thoughts
to put an end
to the lies
but I have yet
to figure it out
and therefore suffer
by the hands
of my own doing

My storms were
nothing but chaos
to you
when all along
I thought
you were the one
holding my umbrella
but you took it
for yourself
and ran for cover
watching the rain
pour around me
like a weatherman
proud of their
correct prediction
you only care
for yourself
and it took me
too long
to realize
those storms
were caused by
your narcissistic hands

I lost myself
in the bottles
the pill bottles
the little blue pills
to fix my crazy
to heal my pain
to ease the sorrow
to calm the anxiety
the pills are generous
in giving me peace
but they stole from me
the one thing
I needed most
my identity
I don't know
who I am
thinking under influence
of a drug
that keeps me
from feeling

How dreadfully
contradicting
it is
that my
biggest fear
is love
but it remains
my greatest
desire

I'm sheltered
but I'm homeless
they kicked me out mentally
saying one thing
and meaning the other
contradicting fools
have driven me mad
I can't do anything right
even when I think
they're on my side
they're really just
playing me with sides
putting me in the middle
unloading their shit on me
as if I were a garbage can
the weight feels unbearable
the pain is hysterical
the headaches are ceaseless
the knot in my stomach
and pressure in my chest
is always there
because of them
if they really cared
like they pretend to
they wouldn't critique
contradict, manipulate or control
every aspect of me
it makes me question
who I am
and what's the purpose
of living
if I'll never amount to anything
more than their dumpster

Everything feels heavy
like my life
is a bag of bricks
I'm carrying
up a mountain
and I can't see
the end
don't know when
I'll feel the release
of pressure again
and at moments
I just want to collapse
close my eyes
sleep the stress away
so that the pain
can't get to me anymore

Eat, drink and smoke
away the misery
and maybe then
you'll qualify as happy
but even those euphorias
don't last too long
before the sadness comes
as if a drape closed
in a once bright room
or a shroud
was placed over the moon
and the sun decided
not to rise
the next day
like some cruel joke
comes the flash of hope
and then snuffed out
like a candle
not allowed to burn
once it's unwanted

I remember that day
home alone
shrouded by the darkness
of my own thoughts
I was putting away dishes
lost in hopelessness
believing I'd be
better off gone
so when
the knife was
in my hand
I held it up
to my chest
trembling under
the weight of voices
determined to die
but just before
the tip of the blade
pierced me
I dropped the knife
and fell to the floor
the sound of
the metal clattering
in my ears
and I became
a heap of tears
drowning
in brokenness
but still alive

Surrounded by
lit candles
with a bottle
of whiskey
and poetry
for company
because you still
don't know
that all of
my thoughts are
about you`

I wake up annoyed
even a beautiful day
can't set me straight
my very thoughts
make me angered
their slight glances
make me flustered
a small sound
makes me perturbed
the whole world
is out to get me
to make my skin crawl
with vexation
this is the irritability
that comes with despair
assuming that the goal
of every day
is to see how bad
you can make it
compared to the last

The truth is
maybe it was
better this way
You taught me alot
like what I
don't want
what I deserve
and you added
extra wounds
broke my heart
but made it
stronger
now I know
what to
watch out for

They're talking about me
I can see the disapproval
in their harsh eyes
feel the judgment
in their cold words
everyone is the enemy
I'll never be fit
for their taste
suited to their standards
tricked into their structure
I protest against their control
but pay the consequence
of always being looked at
as if I were gum on a shoe
a nuisance unable to be ridden of
and I'm glad for my independence
but I feel like the weak prey
who will get attacked
by those swarming hawks
of mindless opinions
all for simply choosing
to be myself
and they wonder
why I'm filled with anguish
but I shouldn't care
for at least
I am who I am

I don't know
if I just didn't care
or if I pretended
that all of my vices
were daily medicines
but I think that
when I became okay
with dying young
I knew that there
was nothing and
no one to blame
but myself
and the pain that
I let haunt me
into thinking that
life wasn't worth it
anymore

I realized that
the reason I'm
never home
and never rest
is because I'm
earnestly searching
for something
magical to happen
as if it would fill
the void of
longing for love
in my chest

Sometimes I think
my words are meaningless
and maybe I should
just stop writing
because most of my poetry
comes from feelings
and feelings are lately
my greatest enemy
because I feel too much
or numb myself
to the point
of not caring
so what's the point…
and then I remember
there's nothing else
I can do
except write

I'm on a rollercoaster
but it's not the fun ride
the theme park thrill
this one I'm on
is deadly
I'm trapped relentlessly
on the slopes
of schizophrenia
my emotions change
like flipping a switch
constantly deluding my sense
causing my loss of sanity
I don't know anything
but the confusion
all the loops and barrels
have made me dizzy
past the point
of walking straight
ever again
if I even
make it off
the rollercoaster
I don't know
who I'd be
so I should stay on

My worst experience
with false hope
was you
because I loved you
more than I had
anyone else
but you strung me along
with all your hopeful lies
I believed in
making me think that
we were meant to last
when your intentions
had always been
to take what you
wanted from me
then cut me off
when I was
no longer of use

If your opinion was wanted
I would've asked for it
but clearly you don't care
you trash who I am
the way I look
the way I act
the very essence
of my soul
and you believe
your harsh words
will change me
but you just
fuel my fire
that burns in rebellion
to make decisions
I'm proud of
but my life
would be peaceful
if you were gone
because even though
I'm strong enough
to fight for myself
there are times
when I'm alone
I feel like
I'm going to break
I hate who I am
and who you are
the anger and sorrow
is too much
on my body
you became the reason
for the cuts
on my wrists

This life feels
like the tires
on a car
it keeps me spinning
until I'm so dizzy
my functioning fails
I lose air
and slowly deflate
barely able to breathe
I am nothing of use
can no longer move
or carry the burden
I'm forced to support
my momentum is gone
there is a puncture
unable to be closed
never to be full again
I'll be stripped apart
piece by piece
and put in a junkyard
discarded to rust
inevitably destroyed
a forgotten void

She used to be
a beautiful flower
until you came
and stole her light
she wilted away
until all her petals fell
because you decided
to break her roots
and let her die
without a drink of water
without a drop of love

My dosage isn't enough
because the stress
has tightened my chest
the bags under my eyes
are from exhaustion
my head aches
from the depression
the anxiety consumes
every emotion
I've spiraled down
the tunnel again
back into the lion's den
stalked by the predators
of fear, despair and
constant worry
they lurk around me in circles
reminding me that the pills
will never fix me
the chaos will never leave me
and no matter how far I run
I can't escape their trap
not until I'm strong enough
to believe in my freedom
to achieve my victory
in silencing those beasts
putting their lies to rest
by ending them all
at the hands of confidence
they took from me

There's been a lot
of hatred
in my heart
towards you
because of all
the verbal abuse
I suffered
you made me believe
I was never
enough for you
or for anyone
but I know
you loved me
in your own way
so I'm sorry
for all the smoke
in my lungs
and the alcohol
in my blood
and the sadness
in my heart
but the broken
parts of me
are wounds from
your weapons

The pressure grows
so severely it burns
I need a distraction
something to ease the pain
to release my clamped jaw
and my clenched fists
I chew piece after piece
of bloody gum
the wretched leak
from my tired cheeks
tastes like salted peppermint
yet I grew to like it
because the bites of power
felt like strikes
on the internal restlessness
the deceiving anxiousness
taking over my body
to become a crippled slave
fearful of my own shadow
unable to use my own voice
chewing gum
all the time
for my panic attacks
I keep extra packs
so I don't look a fool
in their eyes
and I keep
the inner demons
quiet

Just a bit
too brokenhearted
to see the
sunshine today
I know it's there
but the difference is
now I don't
feel it
I only feel
the pain
in my chest
from losing you

Man I'm a mess
lately these nights
I drown out
the world
silence my
own mind
with liquor
get the high
from flower
and tobacco
washing away
my cares
with the lie
of "I'm fine"
and use
the substances
to believe it

See what
they don't
understand is
you can still
fall in love
with someone
without it
being classified
as a relationship
That's why
the heartbreak
is just as bad
when they
decide to
leave you

It must be
both a blessing
and a curse
to feel so deeply
because I'm on
a constant
rollercoaster
unable to catch
my breath
at times
yet I find
it thrilling

Maybe I'll always
be alone
a romanticist that
never finds love
because of fearing
inevitable heartbreak
a poet who writes about romance
because happy endings
are only stories
It's all just a dream
a silver screen infatuation
with the relationships
I'll never have
I've grown up
in the trap
of loneliness
I'm too scared
to let down my walls
because no one would want
the scars beneath them

Coming off the pills
feels like hell
the world is spinning
my stomach churns
but words are coming
easier than before
I'm finally creating
and so I realize
the chaos of my brain
takes me somewhere deep
that the meds took away
This place I go
without the pills
teaches me how
to be a poet again
and I've learned
to love the madness
because of the words
that come without
the pills

I should have
known better
than to trust
someone
who always
made me
wonder
if they
even cared
in the
first place

Fear breaks me
it haunts my mind
like a constant distraction
a demon invading my thoughts
robbing my confidence
taking my identity
and turning me
into a pile of sand
frail and useless
carried away by the wind
scattered into forgotten pieces
lost in oblivion
of eternal regret
and pain of failure
from listening to the lies
I let consume me
fear does not only
take control of your mind
it takes control
of your soul

They'll pick you apart
piece by piece
dissecting every detail
every aspect
of your personality
They'll tell you
how to be
and how to act
making you feel
like you'll never
be good enough
because you're suppose
to meet their standards
be the machine
they programmed you to be
not who you want to be
not letting you taste
the striking flavor
of liberation and identity
It's a tempting treat
they'll lure you with
confusing you to fall
into the trap
because their judgmental words
you listen to
is like them
feeding you
to the sharks
and watching you
get ripped apart
limb by limb
that is their words
they don't care
that you die inside
they don't care
that the sharks attack

Maybe falling in love
is the biggest lie
we tell ourselves
and that's why
it's the worst
kind of pain
having broken
our own trust
to believe in
a fantasy

I know the smoke
in my lungs
is bad for my health
the alcohol in my veins
is breaking me down
and I've gotten more
crinkles around my eyes
from all the stress
and all the damage
I'm causing to
ease the pain
will kill me sooner
but at least
I'm still here
fighting even though
I want it to end

Sometimes I hate myself
for craving danger
because I look for
that exhilaration
in people
but most of the time
those are the ones
that never stay
yet even one night
of adrenaline
is always worth it
for the thrills

It was always
easier for me
to believe
I was a failure
at life
than to
stand back up
after all the rejections
after all the pain
I got knocked down
so many times
I figured out
the best place
for me to be
was on the ground
tucked in a ball
out of everyone's way
because the world
defeated me
and nobody
would miss
a nobody

The sound of
running water
hot to the touch
I remember
the times
when the stress
was so intense
I'd eat until
my stomach
was close to
bursting
and then
turn on
the sink
let the warmth
of the liquid
cover my finger
so it would
easily lodge
down my throat
and I'd throw up
throw up
all the stress
all the food
the calories
worried
about weight
The stress was
out of my control
but throwing up
was gaining control
It was always
a constant
battle
for control

This broken heart
is shielded by
the strong walls
I've locked it in
pretending to be fine
by keeping
all the feelings
stuffed inside
but that's the show
they don't see me
when I'm alone
the complete mess
that I am
the sobbing
the drinking
the smoking
attempting to
numb the pain
and forget
all the memories
for awhile
until it wears off
and I go back
to acting

Sleepless nights
because my mind
is a menace
thoughts lurking
in the shadows
serpent-like
slithering to attack
me as prey
sinking in their teeth
to inject the poison
of fears
and insecurities
toxic enough
to kill
I know this
but often times
the venom
is in my veins
before I can
stop it

I've come to accept
that it's hard
for a fuckup like me
to find romance
I'm the hopeless artist
scarred with the words
of contradicting sides
There is both
light and dark in me
both sane and mad
Life beat me into this
a kind of chaos
I've learned to embrace
but not many can handle
a rose with thorns
because even I know
it's nearly impossible
to break the armor
of thorns I wear
to appear stronger
than I actually am
but if someone ever does
I'll love them until
the last petal falls

The days go
fast and slow
I don't know
the difference anymore
just feel restlessness
throughout my core
my life is a mess
I'm trapped in stress
wanting to escape
but unsure how
to make the break
still stuck now
wishing time away
thinking of sleep
in the day
here comes a creep
sunken eyes
pale skin
half a voice
crazed mind
you thought it all lies
but judgment is a sin
and your choice
to be unkind
is part of the reason
I've lost my mind

Where did
the passion go
It gave me
words to write
instead I stare
at blank pages
and burning candles
wishing a match
was all it took
to rekindle my flame

In the darkest part
of the night
in the deadliest part
of a storm
you left me
with promising words
but took my hope
leaving me vulnerable
to the danger
How could I ever
trust you
when you don't
care enough
to keep my tears
from falling
and chilling me
to the bone

If only I could learn
how to control my thoughts
how to get off
the rollercoaster
of emotions
I'm stuck on
then I wouldn't
need the pills
those little devils
that numb the pain
ought to be
my saviors
but they took away
the most important thing
my creativity
The words have been fleeting
since the dosage
has increased
and it breaks my heart
that I've stopped writing
as much as before
maybe it would be better
to feel the sorrow
without the pills
and be a writer again
than to keep on
living under influence
of medicine
in order to be happy
and less anxious
and in loss
of the one thing
that always held me together
my ability to write

I think us artists
are cursed
with feeling too deeply
At the first sight
of love
we pour our souls
into someone
using all of our
passionate fire
to keep the flames
from going out
We forget
that our feelings
are not always returned
even after we've
handed over our hearts
we can still be rejected
and after becoming attached
to the idea of romance
the most painful thing
of all
is being unwanted
because not only
does our heart and soul break
our energetic spirit
that gives us
the vivacity
to romanticize
starts to die
stealing our creativity
and our ability
to chase after
the very thing
that keeps us alive
Unrequited love
is an artist's
greatest enemy

I bask in
the nighttime
like how one
would lay out
in the sun
because these are
the vulnerable hours
where I make
friends with
the dark
and let it
reveal to me
all of my
brokenness

It's interesting
how love is
the source that
has caused me
the most pain
yet it is
the very thing
I crave most

It's hard
to take care
of yourself
when the parasite
of negativity
inhabits your brain
You stop caring
stop counting
the bottles
and the cigarettes
don't measure
the medicine
don't bother
to even try
and get out
of bed
You'd rather
die
because it's better
than facing reality
but it's not you
that should die
it's that parasite

The most
important lesson
I've ever learned
is that you can't
trust anyone
people will always
let you down
and stab you
in the back
when you're least
expecting it
even the ones
closest to you
are dangerous
because they know
how to make you
believe their lies
That's why I started
embracing my loneliness
because in it
I found the freedom
of knowing that
at least I could
trust myself
but it's very lonely

I try to break out
from the chains
that hold me down
but I'm stuck
no matter how much
I fight the prison
The walls are closing in
and I watch
the end approach
wondering why
I wasted my time
searching for an escape
when I could have learned
to love the madness
I'm trapped in

"To allow myself
to feel
is opening up
my heart
to the rejection
I've always known"
I say
with a lit cigarette
in one hand
and go back
to reading the pages
of a book
to escape the reality
of my heart aching
in the loneliness
I trapped it in

So you need money
to survive
you need a degree
to thrive
but I'd rather live
on an island
alone with my insecurities
than face the reality
that society created
All the selfish greed
is a toxic poison
that only loss
of wealth and things
can heal
I'll live on an island
having little
but gaining
the richest treasure
of all
real liberation

Used to write more
used to laugh more
but I still
wear a smile
so no one sees
just how much
life has
really been
breaking me

Some nights
I'd get so lost
in thoughts
I'd fall into
the trap
of self-hatred
and become
a prisoner
to its lies
I'd stare
in the mirror
with loathing
brushing my teeth
until my gums bled
and my mouth
filled with blood
as if the pain
and the taste
were a punishment
for my insecurities

It's sad
how I think back
to the day
we first met
and laugh at myself
for how stupid
I was
believing that
we'd fall in love
That's the problem
with us writers
we romanticize
on our ideas
fantasize our future
we feel too deeply
get attached too easily
and end up heartbroken
spending months
writing poems
about how unlovable
and alone we feel
some of us
drowning
in pools of alcohol
suffocating
in clouds of smoke
It's a crazy cycle
being a poet
feeling so much
fighting our own mind
so at the hope
of love
we jump

(cont.)

and forget
not everyone
wants to
catch us
This happened to me
with you
and of course
in the end
I lost you

Even if
it kills me
I'll do anything
to experience
even a drop
of magic
to distract me
from this
chaotic
life

I've had depression
for many years
of my life
and I've learned that
there's no cure
it's not in the pills
not in the booze
not in the sex
not in people
not even in religion
there's only accepting it
and deciding to grab it
by the throat
and control it
because the only way
to survive
is to become its master

I feel like
I'm one of those people
with a poisonous touch
The good things
never stay long
It's like I'm toxic
I try to hold on
to a slice of hope
but everything
that crosses my path
soon disappears
along with
my expectations
I'm like a wilted flower
starving for a drink
that never gets more
than a drop
just the tease
of something good

You're such a fighter
winning more battles
than the smiles
you watch from
beneath your armor
and that's why
no one understands
because they don't know
what it's like
to always have to
be strong
on the outside
while in the inside
you're breaking
believing that
nothing else
can save you
except for yourself

I was finally able to
put all of my fears
and insecurities into
a jar on the shelf
but you came
with your words
and shattered it
leaving me to remember
all the things
I tried to forget
while I pick up
the pieces

It's late at night
I'm sitting here
on the floor
listening to jazz
having just released
my built up emotions
in the form of tears
The droplets pour
down my face
like the rain
unwanted, frowned upon
but somehow peaceful
I forget how storms
can bring revival
so I always
make myself fight
to keep my storms away
always think that
I have to be strong
and not feel anything
but it's nights like these
I remember how nice
it is sometimes
to let the rain
just drench me
to release the tears
and feel like a human
alone in a room
full of jazz
and storms
and words

Madness
is a territory
no one wishes
to explore
but yet
they admire
some of the
greatest artists
who were indeed
mad enough
to create
the chaos
that they find
so appealing
Must it be that
it takes someone
who has been to
hell and back
to become such a
great artist

I met an old friend
at a coffee shop
one rainy day
and one of
the first things
he asked me was
"How did you
leave the pit
of depression"
and I responded
"It wasn't until
I learned how
to wake up everyday
grateful to be alive
and healthy
that I learned
true happiness
is not from
what you want
but from what
you already have"
From there I can see
that gratitude
really saved me

I want to be
a butterfly
and shed this cocoon
of old skin
this frail body
has been broken
too many times
it is worn out
from the battle
of fighting sorrow
I yearn
for a transformation
into a new being
a refreshing start
to spread my wings
and learn to fly
to be joyous
without getting
locked in a cage
of despair
ever again
I want to transform
into a butterfly
but keep my scars
as a reminder
not to let
my wings go
to that old skin
Ever again

I've been learning
how to love myself
through every feeling
and moment where
I'm most broken
whether tears are pouring
down my cheeks
or I'm laughing drunkenly
into a cloud of smoke
I love even the
ugly parts of me
because without them
I wouldn't be whole
I wouldn't be human

It's taken me years
to learn that
part of self-love
is being proud
of the things
no one sees...
I'm proud of
all the times
I held it together
when I was breaking inside
all those times
I took care of my parents
when they weren't there for me
all those nights
I finally let myself cry
after staying strong for days
all those smiles I gave
when depression held me captive
all the kindness I showed
when my heart ached in pain
all those times I ate
when I wanted to starve my skeleton
all those times I didn't cut
to reopen the slashes on my wrists
all the times I held a knife
and didn't take my own life
For all of those times
I must remember that I am a fighter
because a lot of times
that's all it took to survive

I've come to realize that all along I was made of glass
as I hunch over my shattered pieces
and try
to figure out where their jagged edges meet
as if I were putting my life back together like a puzzle
my broken fragments spilled before me
like a chaotic mess that's supposed to make a complete picture
of all the things I wish I never said
and all the things I wish I did
of all the ways I wish I never felt
and all the ways I wish I did
of all the things I wish I never did
and all the things I wish I did
and for all that is
and all that is yet to come
I look at the pieces of me
healed together with the glue of my forgiveness
and see myself
as if all along I was a mirror
to my soul
and I see her now
she is strong enough to be standing again

The chaos is fruitful
because it made me
write the truth
I didn't want to share
and even though
vulnerability is the most
uncomfortable form of expression
at least it gave me a purpose
when I didn't feel
like I had one
now I can look back
and see the beauty
in the darkness
the little bits of light
that shown through
took the form of words
and I know that poetry
held me together
when nothing else could
it was the hand
I longed for
to help me
out of the pit
of despair
it was the hand
that helped me
see the light again
and for that
I am forever grateful
and glad to call myself
a poet

www.ingramcontent.com/pod-product-compliance
Lightning Source LLC
Chambersburg PA
CBHW051318120626
46547CB00015B/2287